♥ ♥ ♥ ♥ ♥ ♥ DISCOVER ♥ ♥ ♥ ♥ ♥ ♥ ♥
MIXED-BREED CATS

Trudy Micco

The Cat Fanciers' Association, Inc.® (CFA™) was founded in 1906 as a not-for-profit association of member clubs and is the world's largest registry of pedigreed cats. CFA's mission is to preserve and promote the pedigreed breeds of cats and to enhance the well-being of ALL cats. CFA promotes education, responsible cat ownership, and proper care to the owners of millions of cats worldwide. CFA and its affiliate clubs work nationally with local shelters, at a grassroots level, to help humanely control homeless and feral cat populations, and to encourage voluntary neutering/spaying of pet cats. To learn more about the Cat Fanciers' Association, the pedigreed breeds of cats, or to find the nearest CFA cat show, visit their Web site at www.cfa.org.

Enslow Elementary, an imprint of Enslow Publishers, Inc.

Enslow Elementary® is a registered trademark of Enslow Publishers, Inc.

Library of Congress Cataloging-in-Publication Data

Micco, Trudy.
  Discover mixed-breed cats / Trudy Micco.
    p. cm. — (Discover cats with the cat fanciers' association)
  Includes bibliographical references and index.
  Summary: "Early readers will learn how to care for a mixed-breed
    cat"—Provided by publisher.
  ISBN 978-0-7660-3851-6
  1. Cats—Juvenile literature. I. Title.
  SF442.M53 2012
  636.8—dc22

              2011005896

Future editions:
Paperback ISBN 978-1-4644-0116-9
ePUB ISBN 978-1-4645-1023-6
PDF ISBN 978-1-4646-1023-3

Printed in China

012012 Leo Paper Group, Heshan City, Guangdong, China

10 9 8 7 6 5 4 3 2 1

To Our Readers: We have done our best to make sure all Internet Addresses in this book were active and appropriate when we went to press. However, the author and the publisher have no control over and assume no liability for the material available on those Internet sites or on other Web sites they may link to. Any comments or suggestions can be sent by e-mail to comments@enslow.com or to the address on the back cover.

Every effort has been made to locate all copyright holders of material used in this book. If any errors or omissions have occurred, corrections will be made in future editions of this book.

Photo Credits: Anna Idestam-Almquist/Photos.com, p. 1; Damien Richard/Photos.comp. 8; Erik Clegg/Photos.com, p. 10; © iStockphoto.com/Kim Gunkel, p. 9; © iStockphoto.com/Shelly Perry, p. 6; Mark Chen/Photos.com, p. 18; Olga Miltsova/Photos.com, p. 22; Shutterstock.com, pp. 3, 5, 11, 13, 14, 17, 19, 23.

Cover Photo: Shutterstock.com (tan tabby kitten).

Enslow Elementary
an imprint of
Enslow Publishers, Inc.
40 Industrial Road
Box 398
Berkeley Heights, NJ 07922
USA

http://www.enslow.com

CONTENTS

IS A MIXED-BREED CAT RIGHT FOR YOU?

A **breed** is a type of cat. Mixed-breed cats come in different colors, sizes, and shapes. They can have short hair or long hair. You can find them at **animal shelters**.

Cats go to the bathroom inside a litter box. You should clean the litter every day. Also, empty the box and wash it once a week.

Cats in shelters need good homes.

Older cats can be easier to care for than kittens.

A CAT OR KITTEN?

Most people like kittens. But kittens can be harder to care for than adult cats. They need more attention.

Older cats can be friendlier than kittens at first. Kittens need to get used to being away from their brothers and sisters. Is a kitten or an older cat better for your family?

LOVING YOUR MIXED-BREED CAT

Mixed-breed cats act in different ways. Some may want to be with you all the time. Others may like to be alone. Let your new cat get used to you. You will be friends with him before you know it!

Many cats will let you pick them up and hold them.

Cats like to paw at toys you swing in front of them.

EXERCISE

Some cats will like to lie in the sun.
Others will like to chase after special
cat toys. Get special toys for your new cat
to play with. Playing is exercise for cats.
They need it to stay healthy.

FEEDING YOUR MIXED-BREED CAT

There is wet food and dry food made just for cats. Feed and give your cat fresh water every day. A **veterinarian (vet)**, a doctor for animals, can tell you what kind of food and how much to feed your cat.

Be sure to keep your cat's food and water bowls clean. Dirty bowls can make her sick.

Do not give your cat people food. It can make her sick.

Be gentle when you brush your cat.

GROOMING

Mixed-breed cats can have long hair. Some have short hair. Shorthaired cats can be brushed once or twice a week. Longhaired cats need to be brushed two or more times a week.

Cats scratch on a special post to keep their claws sharp. You can clip their claws once a month. A vet can show you how.

WHAT YOU SHOULD KNOW

Before you bring your new cat home, be sure your home is safe. Some plants are bad for cats.

Cats should not be allowed outside. Cars, mean people, and other animals can hurt them. Cats should stay indoors to stay safe and sound.

Cats enjoy looking out the window when they are indoors.

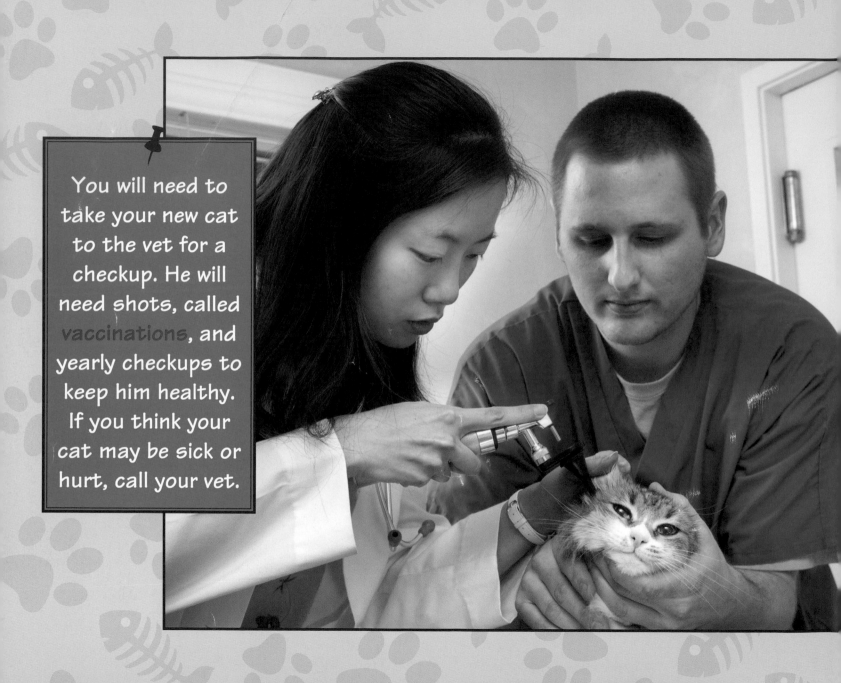

You will need to take your new cat to the vet for a checkup. He will need shots, called vaccinations, and yearly checkups to keep him healthy. If you think your cat may be sick or hurt, call your vet.

A GOOD FRIEND

Your mixed-breed cat will be a good friend to you for many years. Play with him, feed him, and take good care of him.

NOTE TO PARENTS

Mixed-breed cats are special cats and kittens that can be found at local animal shelters and rescue groups. They are also called domestic shorthairs or domestic longhairs. They will each have their own personality. Choose the best one for your family.

Spaying/neutering your cat prior to six months of age is advised. Neutering and spaying will prevent behavioral problems and many life-threatening diseases and help prevent overpopulation.

To keep your cat safe, keep him indoors. It is also a good idea to microchip your cat, in case he gets lost. A vet will implant a microchip under the skin that contains your contact information, which can then be scanned at a vet's office or animal shelter. Some towns require licenses for cats, so be sure to check with your town clerk. Also, check your home for potential dangers. Some plants and foods are toxic to cats. String can be very dangerous too. Cats like to play with it and sometimes they will eat it, which can cause them to get very sick and require surgery to remove. Ask your vet or visit www.cfa.org for a full list of concerns and for cat-proofing ideas.

Some things you will need before bringing your new cat home:

- **litter box** (Veterinarians recommend more than one in different places in the house.)

- **litter** (There are many brand choices.)

- **water and food bowls** (Use stainless steel, glass, crock, or other nonplastic material.)

- **cat food** (Ask the shelter or your veterinarian to recommend a good quality food. The better quality the food, the healthier the cat, which means fewer trips to the vet's office.)

- **cat bed** (Select something the cat can snuggle into.)

- **special cat toys** (Select safe toys that do not have small parts or string that could come off and injure your cat.)

- **grooming brushes**

- **cat nail clipper** (or a human toenail clipper)

- **scratching posts** (There should be a few in different easily accessible locations in the house to keep the cat from damaging furniture.)

- **carrier** (Make sure your cat can stand up and move around in the carrier as an adult.)

animal shelter—A place where unwanted kittens and
cats live before going to good homes.

breed—A type of cat.

litter box—A special box where cats go to the bathroom.

vaccination—A shot that cats need to stay healthy.

veterinarian (vet)—A doctor for animals.

Books

Kalman, Bobbie. *Baby Cats.* New York, N.Y.: Crabtree Pub., 2008.

Tourville, Amanda Doering. *Purr and Bounce: Bringing Home a Cat.* Minneapolis, Minn.: Picture Window Books, 2009.

Internet Addresses

The Cat Fanciers' Association: For Kids
<http://kids.cfa.org/>

ASPCA Kids
<http://www.aspca.org/aspcakids/>

INDEX